Six Steps to Successful Self-Publishing

SIX
STEPS
to SUCCESSFUL
Self-Publishing

A BEGINNER'S GUIDE

PATRICIA MARSHALL

LUMINARE PRESS

WWW.LUMINAREPRESS.COM

Six Steps to Successful Self-Publishing
A Beginner's Guide
© 2019 Patricia Marshall

Printed in the United States of America

Cover Design: Melissa K. Thomas

Luminare Press
442 Charnelton St.
Eugene, OR 97401
www.luminarepress.com

ISBN: 978-1-64388-125-6

Contents

A Note from the Author

This book offers an overview of the self-publishing process and attempts to capture current best practices in an ever-evolving industry.

At Luminare Press, we constantly review our resources—including news sites, blogs, industry events, and more—to keep up to date with the latest in the publishing world. We want to give our clients the most current options in order to enhance their publishing experience and offer the best cost-saving options.

Six Steps to Successful Self-Publishing is a print-on-demand book, which allows me to update and revise when information changes or when we find improvements.

If you are reading this and find either errors or out-of-date information, please feel free to contact me. A second edition is only a few clicks away.

—Patricia Marshall

Self-Publishing Overview

If you are a writer, I have both good news and bad news.

First, the good news: You can become a published author! Thousands of writers just like you are writing, publishing, and selling books without having an agent, editor, or publisher. They're using print-on-demand (POD) to make paper books, and electronic formats to make ebooks, and you can too.

Print-on-demand and electronic books have upended the publishing industry and opened the door to tremendous opportunities for writers to introduce their work to the world.

Print-on-Demand and ebooks offer affordable options for an author who wants to self-publish. Unlike the not-so-distant past, when most books were created through offset printing (which involved huge print runs to make the cost of the book affordable), POD books are produced from high-quality PDF files. This allows books to be printed one at a time for a reasonable print cost.

Paired with a distribution system that allows POD and electronic books to be sold through the same system and in the same locations as traditionally published books, self-published books can be created and distributed in a way that makes them virtually indistinguishable from any other type of book. This is nothing short of revolutionary. Now the bad news: Being a financially successful author is going to be a challenge.

Self-publishing, once considered the last resort for desperate writers, has gained not only a broad acceptance but has, in some cases, become the stuff of myth. Successful self-published authors—Amanda Hocking (*My Blood Approves*, The Hollows Series), Hugh Howey (*Wool*, The Silo Series), E.L. James (*Fifty Shades of Grey*), to name a few—have created the illusion that all you have to do is put your work out and fame and fortune will be instantaneous. Even authors who may have an opportunity to attract traditional publishing deals have started making the choice to self-publish and retain control of their work and their royalties.

Thanks to the ease with which any author can make his or her work available for sale—and fueled by tales of self-publishing success—the market is flooded with self-published print and electronic books of all types: first-time novels, fantasy and sci-fi series, nonfiction stories, memoirs, children's picture books, young adult novels, poetry, business, and how-to books.

In 2015, Bowkers Books in Print reported that 625,000 books were self-published. If you want to join the crowd, you are going to have a lot of competition. And if you want to be successful, you're going to face a lot of challenges. After all, if anyone with a computer and the Internet can create a book almost overnight, how do you convince readers that YOUR product is the result of the hard work you've put into it?

Unfortunately, many self-published efforts fall short. In one case, the content might be stellar, but the book design is poor and the cover amateurish; in another, a great story gets lost in a sea of typos. In many cases, self-published books fail to find their target—the reading public.

But it's possible to self-publish a book that is virtually indistinguishable from a traditionally published book. With a little effort and attention and an understanding of where you might need help along the way, it's possible to turn your manuscript into a professional, polished book whose content and look rival any book out there without breaking your budget.

Most authors approach self-publishing with stars in their eyes. By its very title, self-publishing sounds like a do-it-yourself project, something that might take a few weeks but certainly nothing a book-loving individual couldn't tackle. If you've lived with books your whole life and are a reasonably smart, literate person (most writers I know are) it's easy to rationalize that the process of making a book couldn't be that hard.

But when you decide to publish your work, you become part of a long tradition of bookmaking. As part of that tradition, you need to understand the basics of the profession so you can deliver a product that lives up to the standards of the industry and your audience's expectations.

It's important to understand that publishing and writing are distinct disciplines. Not to say that there aren't commonalities—both professions worship words and appreciate books to the point of obsessiveness. But just as there are authors who spend their whole lives working to perfect the art of storytelling, there are editors, graphic designers, and text and font geeks who are working to perfect theirs. And neither profession can be picked up in an afternoon or fully assimilated in a month.

Beyond the book design aspect, if you plan to self-publish your work, you need to devote time and energy to understanding the basic language of the business, to recognizing what tasks are beyond your skill set, and to knowing when and how to find professionals to help. The subsequent chapters will break down the publishing tasks and provide a step-by step overview of the process.

Almost everything I tell you will apply to any publishing method you choose. Although many people want to believe that publishing an ebook is a shortcut, the savvy author will realize that almost everything that applies to print books applies to ebook, except the final output. We'll discuss the steps of making a book that will reach the reading public—and how to find an audience.

Whether you decide to take on publishing on your own, hire someone to do the whole thing, or choose something in-between, you are going to have to familiarize yourself with the process. The mechanics of bookmaking are the same for almost every author, and in the following chapters, we'll discuss each step in detail.

A Brief Overview of the Publishing Process

- Print-on-Demand (POD) books are published from files the author or publisher submits to a printer. To **publish a print book**, you are going to have to create and then upload two files to a POD printer: an interior, which is the body of the book, and a cover file, which will include back cover and spine. Your files must conform to the standards set by the printer.

- Ebooks are distributed from files that the author provides to ebook distributors. To **publish an ebook**, you will need to format your document as an HTML file, then convert it to an e-pub, according to ebook standards, create a cover file (front only), and upload your cover and interior file to ebook distribution sites. There are several ebook formats; you will need to know which sites accept which formats and be sure you have all formats available.

- **For both formats**, all the elements—including editing, cover design and text formatting—need attention in order to make a product conform to readers' expectations.

- Also for both formats, and to make the book is discoverable (and therefore salable), you are going to have to **ensure that the proper metadata** is in place, which means you will register your book with Bowker Books in Print, get an ISBN and barcode, set the retail price, and make sure your book description, key words, and channels are set up properly.

- Along with publishing, the self-publishing author needs to have a basic understanding of how book marketing works. Unlike the field of dreams, your audience will not materialize just because you've put your work out in the world. If you want to find an audience and generate some income, you will need to create **a realistic plan to sell and market your book.** Marketing should start long in advance of publishing, and while it can be challenging for an author, it can also be a fun and rewarding part of the writing experience, especially when it comes to interacting with readers.

What's Next

Self-publishing a book takes a lot of work and knowledge, but once you understand the process, you can break it down into manageable portions and decide how much you want to tackle on your own. In the following chapters, I'm going to give you details about each of these steps, along with suggestions about how and when to approach each.

In **Chapter Two**, we'll cover manuscript preparation. This chapter will help you determine what level of editing your manuscript needs, determine who will do it, incorporate changes and edits, polish the manuscript, and prepare for book layout.

Chapter Three will focus on the interior of the book and guide you as you determine the size of the book, look of the page, how you will create the interior file, what program you will use, front and back matter, including copyright, author bio, acknowledgments, title page, and any other information that is separate from the body of your story.

Chapter Four focuses on the cover, including basic elements of cover design, and guidelines for creating a compelling cover that fits your genre; writing back cover text; finding and licensing images; working with a cover designer; and preparing files for upload.

Chapter Five covers the mechanics of publishing, including printing, distribution, and ebook options. It explains just what the heck metadata is and how you can make sure that the proper information about your book is in place and how to make your book available through multiple channels

Chapter Six will offer suggestions for setting up a marketing plan that works for you in order to reach an audience and sell your book. We'll talk about easy steps you can take on your own and when it might be time to call a professional to help you build a community of readers for your work.

The Perfect Words:
From Manuscript to Layout

The first step on the road to publishing (after writing a book, of course) focuses on one process: editing. You know, the glamorous stuff: grammar, punctuation, proper spelling, etc. If you are serious about getting a professional book published, then you should consider hiring a professional editor to review the text.

"But my spouse is an English teacher," you say. Or, "My writing group has been through this forward and backward ,and they are like the grammar police—there's no way there are mistakes in this book."

You know what's coming next, don't you? I'm going to tell you that you are wrong.

Family members, friends, writing groups—they are all invaluable when it comes to reading and critiquing your manuscript. But they are not a replacement for a professional who reads manuscripts for style, consistency, grammar, punctuation, and much, much more.

Producing a book that meets the standards of the book industry (and the readers' expectations) requires, at a minimum, a professional copyedit and thorough proofreading before the book is printed. Self-published authors often overlook these crucial steps, but as publishing professionals, we know that no matter how talented an author you are, your work needs to be edited before you commit it to print.

Hiring an editor may seem like a big expense—in fact, it may be the biggest expense of the whole process—but it's not a place to skimp.

Traditional publishing houses employ an army of copyeditors and proofreaders because they understand that no writer has enough distance to proof and correct his or her own work. If you are self-publishing, you need to take the same approach. Your book must be free of errors and stylistically in tune with similar books in order for it to be competitive in the market.

Types of Editing

"Editing" is a huge—and sometimes subjective—term. Content editors will have a different approach than copyeditors, so it's good to familiarize yourself with the type of editing your manuscript requires before you proceed with the process.

For my clients, I break down the process into three types of edits and proofreading. The distinction between the three is not always cut and dry, as there is certainly some overlap, but it's good to be aware of what you are looking for, so you can make informed decisions as you determine what your manuscript might need or benefit from.

Copyediting is the process of going through the text and paying attention to the minutia. Copyeditors correct spelling, grammar, punctuation, syntax, and sometimes word usage, though competent editors are careful to preserve the meaning and voice of the original text. They are paying attention to homonyms (there and their, who's and whose), comma placement, dashes, and a host of grammar issues that are easy to overlook. They also are reading the text for consistency and to impose style and format if required. This includes such things as when and how numbers are spelled out, capitalization of certain words, or unusual punctuation or spelling that is unique to your particular manuscript. In addition, most copyeditors will query the author about redundancies, apparent errors, or inconsistencies. Some will fact check text or at least question dates, titles, and names that seem off-kilter.

Line editing often encompasses copyediting but is a more substantial examination of the manuscript in order to identify and solve problems of overall clarity or accuracy. Line editors may suggest reorganization of the text, either by paragraph, sections, or chapters to improve the flow. They may suggest verbiage changes by writing or rewriting segments or may offer text revisions for any and all of the text. They will point out concerns (inconsistent character attributes, for example) and may suggest solutions or assist an author in the process of rewriting if necessary.

Developmental, or content editing is big-picture editing of a draft or nearly complete manuscript. This is what most writers think of when they think of an editor associated with a publishing house. Generally, a developmental editor will work with the author on any and all aspects of the manuscript, including analyzing the overall structure of the manuscript, the clarity and voice, character development, plot, or use of tenses. Developmental editors are often involved during the writing process, and they guide the author during writing and rewriting the text. Most self-publishing authors will not work with a developmental editor but will have friends, family, or writing group members who function as guides for the book development.

Proofreading is the process of reading the "proof" of a book that is printed to be reviewed before publication for typos or any other errors in the text. Proofreading is usually the last step before going to press and is done in addition to editing.

Before you seek out an editor, you need to understand what type of editing your manuscript needs and confirm that you are hiring an editor whose work is in alignment with your expectations.

How to Find and Hire a Copyeditor

Good copyeditors are not like you and me. Their brains are wired to see anomalies, deviations, and inconsistencies in the text. Whether they're spotting errors in the church program, the menu, or the novel they just purchased, they'll be itching to get their hands on a red pen. They read the *The Chicago Manual of Style*—in bed, at night, for fun—and can explain to you (not that you want to know) the difference between and em- and en-dash or how to properly punctuate and abbreviate Great Britain Pounds.

We are lucky to have them in our midst. A good copy-editor will make sure that your book meets professional standards and will keep you from publishing a book with embarrassing mistakes.

Editors can be found all sorts of ways. There are professional editing groups such as the Editorial Freelancers Association and the American Copy Editors Society. Several of these are listed in the resource page.

It's worth taking some time to find an editor who meets your needs and is a good fit for you. It's important that before you hire an editor, you and your editor agree on the work to be done, and following these guidelines may ensure that you are on the same page (as it were).

- Agree on a price per word or per page. If you agree on a page price, each page should be formatted in Times New Roman, 12 point, with one-inch margins on all sides. There's no point in paying more if you like to work in a larger font, and, conversely, you shouldn't try to decrease the page number by using a small font or narrow margins.

- Request a sample edit of five or ten pages. If you have questions about the edits or disagree with the editor's approach or scope, discuss it with them BEFORE they continue.

- Agree on a stylebook to use as a guide. Book editors typically use *The Chicago Manual of Style*, but you may have a technical or specialized manuscript that calls for a different type of stylebook.

- Request that the editor provide a final style sheet specific to your manuscript. This should include a list of proper names, unusual spellings, and any style or formatting issues particular to the manuscript.

- Agree on a format for markup—will the editor make corrections and give you notes using Track Changes (a Microsoft Word feature that allows changes within a document to be tracked and reviewed)? Will he or she print the manuscript and make notes by hand? Who will be responsible for the final text?

- Determine who will proofread the book before publication. Many authors do this themselves or ask friends or family members to go through the printed book.

As you are seeking editors, be sure to ask for referrals, and check with other clients to see if the editor met their expectations, both time and money-wise.

It's important that your editor knows what you are asking for and that you agree on how you would like him or her to input changes.

Once your manuscript is edited, you will have to go through it again to review the edits, if it's done manually, and enter the changes. If it's done electronically, you'll need to accept or reject the changes.

You don't have to accept all the edits—there may be some that you disagree with or that you feel change the meaning of what you're saying. But do consider that an editor is an intelligent, noninvested first reader, and give appropriate weight to his or her suggestions.

Lastly, be aware that even if you hire a professional

editor, it is unlikely that one pass on your manuscript will catch all the errors. It's possible to introduce errors as you accept or reject changes, and I think it's important that you—and possibly a proofreader—go through the book at least once after it is laid out. When I was a magazine editor, I calculated that every piece that went to print had been reviewed a minimum of twenty-three times total in the process from manuscript to print. Some of those were the same sets of eyes in different stages. It took a lot of reviewing to get it right.

Suggestions for Self-Editing

If hiring an editor is absolutely out of the question and you cannot trade for services or bribe one, I am including a few tips for self-editing, in no particular order, that you might find useful.

Grammar, punctuation, and layout:

- Spell check will not catch everything, but don't skip running it. And consider using a search feature to look for things like double punctuation marks (periods, commas, etc.), quote marks followed immediately by a period, or other odd text anomalies.

- Place punctuation (periods, commas, etc.) inside quotes, in almost every case.

- Be consistent with capitalization in chapter titles and subheads.

- When you are reviewing, be sure to turn on the spelling and grammar controls in your word processing program (usually under system preferences), and pay attention when you see green or red squiggly lines under a word or phrase. Think of those lines as queries: You may have made a deliberate word choice that the computer flags, but it may be something you need to fix.

- When writing dialogue, remember: new speaker, new paragraph.

- Punctuate to control the reading experience and guide the reader.

Writing tone, voice, and rhythm:

- Watch out for "to be" verbs: is, was, am, are—they convey no action. Instead, animate your text with active, strong verbs. "To be" verb forms have a place, but too many will drag your prose down.

- Vary sentence length—it makes the rhythm and pace of your writing so much more enjoyable. Sentences that are similar in length are boring. Try breaking them up, using short ones to punctuate a paragraph or add a surprising twist.

- Avoid excessive adjective or adverb use. Adjective and adverbs have their place, but too many of them make the text feel overwritten. In fact, you can remove most adverbs (descriptive words that end with -ly) without changing the meaning of your text.

- Avoid clichés. They are one of my biggest writing blunders. Search them out and destroy them, unless absolutely necessary.

- Avoid excessive clauses, particularly a string of them in a row. Instead, consider breaking one sentence into two.

- Be inventive with word choice but not for the sake of being inventive: Don't write like you've been reading a thesaurus.

- Root out diminutives, unnecessary qualifiers, and waffling descriptors: a little, a bit, very, could have been, sort of, kind of, etc. They make your writing feel weak and tentative.

There are a lot of good resources available about the writing and editing process, but one of the best suggestions I can offer a writer when it comes to revising text is to read it out loud. Yes, your neighbors/family members/coworkers might think you are crazy, but reading your work out loud allows you to hear the rhythm and flow, uneven pacing and sentence construction, repetitive words, and more. Adjust as necessary.

Turning the Page

Once you have your manuscript edited and ready to publish, you need to create the interior book pages. Sometimes referred to as a "book block," your final product will be a PDF file, which you will upload for printing.

There are a number of ways you can go about making the interior of your book. Budget-minded authors may choose to download one of the many free or low-cost templates available online. Some will tackle the layout themselves using Microsoft Word. Others will hire a designer to lay out the pages (generally done with InDesign). In any case, and whatever program is used, the end result must be a PDF file of the interior pages of your book. There are pros and cons to all the options listed above.

> **Templates:** There are several sources of book interior templates available; costs run from free to several hundred dollars. Most (but not all) free templates require you to use the printing and publishing services of the provider (which might not always be a bargain). If you are purchasing a template, you must make sure the program is compatible with programs you have. Templates are a workable option for a DIY author, but they don't offer a perfect solution. While templates can be custom-

ized, they are still templates and will not allow you the freedom of design that marks a wonderful book. And if you have complicated formatting or images in the text, you may find yourself extremely frustrated with the process of trying to apply predetermined styles to an unconventional layout.

Word: Some authors choose to create their book in a text program such as Microsoft Word. These programs are not intended as a design and layout format, but with meticulous attention to detail, it's possible to make your book interior in a text program. Some downsides: Text layout will not be as smooth as it will in design software; pagination, headers, and footers can be tricky.

On the plus side, most authors are familiar with the mechanics of Word and can stumble through the process of laying out the book themselves, provided they have some technical expertise and a reserve of patience. Like templates, however, if your formatting is complex or you have a lot of images, Word is not your best option.

InDesign: Professional design software, such as InDesign, is difficult for nondesigners to master. It is also expensive, and though it's available as a subscription (around $20 a month at this printing) if you're not familiar with it, you are going to have to subscribe for a while. You will also need an operating system that can handle it and a working knowledge of cloud storage.

InDesign is a deep program that will deliver a solid, professional product. The software handles text elegantly, offers wider design choices, and generally allows more options when it comes to layout and design. Style changes are easy to implement; master pages allow for universal application of the look. Also, in the hands of someone who is familiar with the program, the process should be much quicker than other layout options.

A note: It may seem tempting to subscribe to Creative Cloud for a few months in order to master InDesign basics and lay out your book. Don't do this unless you are considering a second career as a graphic designer. The time you will put into mastering the program is guaranteed to bring you nothing but headaches, and as an amateur, your book may be worse off than it would be had you stuck to Word.

Hiring a designer: You may find that you'd rather just put your book in the hands of a professional. The obvious drawback to this is cost. Book interiors can run anywhere from several hundred to thousands of dollars. A couple things to note if you decide to go this route: Find someone who has designed books before—there's a lot more to it than meets the eye, and even experienced designers will have a learning curve if they've not done it before. Second, be aware that if you have edits after you've had a chance to proof the book, your designer will have to correct the text, so you may incur additional charges. Be wary if someone is offering this for a price that seems too good to be true. It probably is and will lead to headaches later on. The upside is a professional-looking book interior.

Before you tackle any of these options, you need to determine what size the book will be. POD sizes are for "trade" paperbacks, and standard sizes are 5 x 8, 5.5 x 8.5 and 6 x 9. There are other sizes available, and you should check the specs of the company with whom the book is to be printed. Most novels and memoirs, poetry, and other nonfiction will fall into the sizes above. If you are in doubt about sizes, take a ruler and measure some books on your shelf. Trade paperbacks will mostly fall into that category. Mass market paperbacks—the smaller books often known as pocket books—are not an option for POD.

Whatever option you choose, you should familiarize yourself with what the interior of a book should look like. The basic elements of a page include the header and footer, the page number (or folio), and the text body. The first page in a chapter will include a chapter title and/or number, and the first paragraph of a chapter is often styled a little differently. If your book is broken into sections, you will have section pages with titles and/or section numbers. Many books have scene breaks within chapters, noted by a couple of blank spaces with or without some type of design between the paragraphs. The first paragraph of a new scene is often styled differently.

Some guidelines:

- For the main text, particularly if this is your first attempt, stick with a standard font that's suitable for books. I recommend Garamond, Minion, Palatino, or Caslon. You can't go wrong with one of those. For your chapter and section titles, you can be more creative, but be sure the font is readable and pleasing to the eye.

- Keep the body font at 12 points or at least close to it. Too large, and it will look oversized; too small and it will be difficult to read. Chapter and section titles can be larger, of course. If the page feels crowded, try to adjust the leading (the distance from the baseline of the text to the next baseline) to be a little larger. Most programs will automatically set leading at 1.2 of the font size (14.4 for a 12 pt font), but increasing it can make the page a little more breathable.

- Body text should be justified on both right and left sides. That means the margins will be straight, unlike a Word document with ragged right edges.

- The beginning of each paragraph should be indented, and you should not put an additional space or paragraph return after a paragraph. Often paragraphs at the start of a chapter or after a break are not indented, and the first after a chapter title may use a drop cap or some other style.

- Don't squeeze text on the page. Leave sufficient margins (the inside, or spine side, should be wider than the outside) and headers to give your words a little breathing room. If the text seems too dense to you, try to adjust the leading, as mentioned above.

- Correctly place headers, footers, and page numbers. If the author name, title, or page number are in the header, be sure to delete or move that information to the footer on chapter opening pages. Never have a header or footer on a blank page or a section page.

- Paginate correctly. Odd-numbered pages are on the right (recto) page, even pages on the left (verso). Start your text (or introduction) on page one, even though there are pages before that. It's not necessary to include page numbers on front and back material, though in some cases an author may choose to.

- Speaking of front and back matter, be sure to include a title page, copyright page, and table of contents, if you are using one. Some books also have acknowledgments, a preface or introduction in the front and appendices, author information, and an epilogue in the back. *The Chicago Manual of Style* has a suggested order for books that is worth reviewing.

First Impressions: The Cover

You know the old saying, never judge a book by its cover? I've got some news for you: Everyone judges a book by its cover.

The cover offers the first impression of your book to most readers, and if you're self-publishing, you will be wise to invest time, energy, and possibly money in it. With the barrage of information flashing by us every day, your book cover is your first chance to grab a reader, and you don't want to squander that opportunity.

You've probably been imagining your book cover for a long time. Once you decide to self-publish, you have to get down to the basics of cover design, which means paying attention to the details that go into making your perfect idea a reality.

Creating an Appealing Cover

When it comes to determining your cover design, other books offer a readily available guide. Go to your shelves or a bookstore, and start to browse. Take some time to really examine all of the elements of a cover, particularly those that are in a genre similar to yours. Make note of what you like and don't, what elements are common, and how each cover appeals to you.

There are three basic cover areas to consider: the front, the back, and the spine.

The front cover includes a cover image, the book title, author name, sometimes a subtitle, a brief line about the story, and/or a testimonial.

The spine has the book title, author name, and the publisher's logo.

The back cover may contain any or all of the following: a book description, an author picture and brief biography, testimonials, barcode and ISBN, book price, and publisher logo.

It's important to note here that one of your goals with the cover will be to have it look as if it belongs with other books of its type or genre. Romance novels have a particular look and feel that is inappropriate to noir fiction or horror stories. Nonfiction and literary fiction have a broader range, but they still generally have covers that announce what they are, as do young adult novels. As you look at covers in your genre, you'll notice these distinctions.

There's design variation within each genre, of course, but when you are considering your own cover, don't stray too far. Many amateur publishers make the mistake of thinking that they need to do something unique and original to make their cover stand out, but this is the place to exercise a little restraint—you can make a great, creative cover that appeals but also fits in.

I have a few front cover rules that I employ for the books I publish. Aside from being genre appropriate, I recommend the following:

- Make the cover text strong and easy to read at a small scale—most readers will first see the book online, at about an inch or inch and a half wide. You want them to be able to read your title at this size.

- Limit the images and ideas that you are asking the reader to absorb. If you crowd your cover with significant book elements, use imagery to make visual puns, or use a symbolic image that makes no sense unless you have read the book, you're missing an opportunity. A strong, central visual element, elegantly married to the text, is your best bet.

- Use appropriate, readable fonts. Fancy fonts can jam things up or can be difficult to read. And ho-hum fonts (hello, Times New Roman and Papyrus!) are just boring and the sure sign of an amateur design. Remember: your cover should be creative, yet suitable to your genre and readable.

And remember, the cover is not a place for clever wordplay—you have a whole book for that, so keep any cover text clean and approachable.

Once you have developed an idea that works with your genre and is clear, it's time to execute the design. This may be one of the best times to employ a professional. Even though cover design can be costly, if you expect your book to have commercial success, it will be well worth it.

There are a lot of designers out there, but I'll offer these guidelines on finding and working with a designer.

- Look for a designer who has done book covers before. There's a protocol and process to making a book cover, and you will save time and possibly expensive mistakes if you work with someone who is experienced.

- Convey your idea to your designer by providing samples of covers you like, images you would like to use, and colors you prefer. Let him or her know what you envision, but don't get married to anything in particular—designers can take your direction and come up with something that you haven't even thought of but is just what you want.

Supplying clear and final information to the designer should save you time and money. Providing cover art (if you have it), book title, subtitle, author name as you would like it to appear, back cover text, author bio, and picture in the beginning will help the process.

If you're stuck on images ideas, try Googling a few terms (be sure to hit the "image" button in the Google search bar) and provide links to possible pictures.

Things that will increase the cost of cover design will be requests for original illustration, having the designer hunt for images, or choosing expensive stock images. I've listed several relatively inexpensive photo banks at the end of this chapter—be sure to keep your eye on the prices so you don't fall in love with one that's out of your range.

If you already have an image—a family photo, a piece of art, or something else—that's great, but it's not a substitute for cover design. A picture is not a book cover. It's an element that can be used on the cover. You'll supply that picture to a designer, who will craft a cover that incorporates it.

Back Cover Text

Back cover text should be written in a way that advertises the book to a potential reader, so in that sense, it's more like marketing writing than prose writing. While the details of your character's origin story might be compelling and imperative for the reader to understand, the back cover is no place to tell that story—it's the place to summarize the plot in a way that will grab the readers' attention and make them want to buy the book.

Back cover text is often the hardest text for an author to write. Authors are so close to their plot and their characters that they have difficulty writing in broad strokes. Back cover text is not intended to be a synopsis of the book, nor does it need to be detailed. This text stands as a promise to the reader: in these pages you will find (fill in the promise). The origin story may be appropriate, but an unbiased third party is probably the best judge of that.

It's hard for me to put my finger on exactly what elements comprise a successful back cover—it's more like I know it when I see it—but here are some things to consider:

- A headline, styled a little differently than the main text, is attention grabbing.

- Keep the following paragraphs short, and use simple, clear language.

- Write in third person. Remember, this is not the place for explaining "why I wrote this book." You want the reader to be intrigued by the story, not bogged down by your motivation.

- For nonfiction, in particular, consider breaking up text by using bullet points or different styles—you want the reader to be able to scan quickly for the main points of your book.

- Resist exclamation points. They can work sometimes, but you're probably better off without them.

- Also avoid bold or underlined text. It just looks wrong.

- Show, don't tell, with text that will make the reader want to open the book.

- DO NOT tell the reader in the back cover text that they won't be able to put the book down, or that it's a page turner (see the previous point). It's much better to let a third party say these things.

Other Back Cover Elements:

Blurbs: Some authors have testimonials, or blurbs, from people about how wonderful the book is. Blurbs are nice, but the speaker should be someone whose position or title makes them at least a tangential expert on the topic. Having a blurb from Ann Smith, your neighbor, is not particularly powerful (though you can encourage Ann to leave a review on Amazon or Goodreads, as we'll discuss in the next chapter). Be sure your reviewer is speaking from a position of knowledge.

Author photo and biography: If your biography is on the back, you should keep it short and stick to the elements that pertain to the book. This is not a resume, just a brief note about your relevant experience to the story. This, too, should be in third person.

Barcode, ISBN, and price: Most printers will supply a barcode; ISBNs can be obtained through Bowkers Books in Print (more on this in the next chapter).

When it comes to the cover of your book, pay attention. Consumers might not know what goes into good cover design, but they'll know what's not good, and they'll pass right by it.

So be sure that your cover is one that will grab the readers rather than one that makes it easy for them to move on.

Printing, Distribution, and Metadata

You will encounter the term metadata frequently in the publishing world. Don't let it scare you. Metadata is simply information about your book. As a self-publisher, you will be asked to provide metadata when you upload your files to be printed, apply for your ISBN, and more, and you need to ensure that the information is consistent and accurate.

To do this, create a metadata sheet on which to enter all the data you gather. Do this AT THE BEGINNING—don't count on being able to remember the details.

A good metadata sheet equips you with a record of information you will use throughout the publishing process. You won't have all this information when you start, but as you get new data, you can add it to the sheet.

Here's a list and explanation of most of the elements:

Book title and subtitle: Be sure to note if you use an ampersand instead of "and" or any other symbols. Capitalization, spelling, punctuation, and proper names should be consistent.

Author name: If you use your middle name or initial, or a nickname, note it so you always identify yourself the same way.

Book specs: Keep note of type of book (hardback, soft-cover, color) along with paperweight and color, if you have an option.

Number of pages: This, along with the other book specs, will determine your spine width, shipping weight, and printing cost. This refers to the TOTAL number of pages, not just the numbered pages. You won't have this information until the book interior is finished.

Book size: You should have the front cover dimensions early in the design process. Add the spine width once you have it.

Book shipping weight: This information will be available through the printer once the book specs are complete.

ISBN: Books are identified with a 13-digit number called an ISBN (international standard book number.) You get an ISBN through Bowker or through your printer.

Library of Congress number: A Library of Congress number is not required, but record it if you have one.

Publication date: Record the date the book is available for sale.

Book description: Many authors use back cover text or a variation of it as a book description. Keep track of your book description. Publishing platforms, including ebook sites, will have a place to enter it. For more on this, see the previous chapter on cover design.

Key words: Create a list of keywords related to your book topic. Enter them in the keyword fields. Keep track of what you have used.

Target audience: Adult trade is common for novels and nonfiction, but other categories may be appropriate.

Category: Record the book categories you've chosen.

Other Information

ISBN: You can buy one through Bowker for $125, or ten for $295. Some publishers, Luminare Press included, supply authors with an ISBN. Some online printers, such as KDP or IngramSpark, will provide a free one, but be sure that there are no restrictions on it. If you get one yourself, either directly from Bowker or from an online printer, you will need to supply your book information to Bowker (they have a form online to fill out.)

Library of Congress: You can register your book with the Library of Congress at ecips.loc.gov. There is no charge to register your book, but you will need to send a copy to the Library of Congress once the book is published.

Copyright: You can claim copyright on your work simply by including the copyright symbol (©) before your name on the copyright page of your book. Some authors choose to go through a more formal process of copyright by registering the book at copyright.gov. There is a small fee to register online, and you may be required to send a book.

Understanding Book Economics

I frequently have authors ask about cost of production and author royalties, but the answer is never simple or short. As a self-publishing author, you need to have a basic understanding of book economics and associated terms. It can be confusing, but the more you know, the more it will make sense.

Costs associated with the book production:

Files: Making the cover and interior PDFs from which your book will be printed. This is a one-time cost and encompasses the process we've talked about so far.

Printing: Printing costs are the actual cost to produce your book once the files are in place. With POD, the cost of printing the book is incurred every time you sell a book or order copies from the printer. Your printing costs will be driven by the length of book (number of pages), the size, the type of binding, and whether the interior is color or black and white. If you choose not to use POD, the number of books you produce will also be a cost factor.

Sales cost: If a third party—Amazon, Barnes and Noble, or an indie bookstore—sells your book, they expect to get a sales discount. The sales discount is a percentage of the retail cost. There are a lot of different opinions about discount percentages; I set my books with a 55 percent discount, which is the industry standard.

Marketing: You should factor in marketing costs for your book, whether it is as simple as free books for influential readers or as complex as an ongoing advertising campaign.

Royalties: Royalties are the portion of the book sale that an author receives after the printing costs and sales discounts are deducted. Some self-publishing companies take a royalty percentage, just as a traditional publisher would. Some (including Luminare Press) give authors 100 percent of royalties.

So if you buy a book yourself to sell to family, friends, or at a reading or book fair, you would pay the printing and shipping cost from the printer, and sell it for the retail cost (or at a discount; it's your choice). If your book has a $10 cover price and printing and shipping are $3, you would make $7 when sold at retail.

A third-party seller will take a sales discount, usually between 40 and 55 percent. So, using the same model above, you would give a seller between $4 and $5.50, deduct the printing cost, and the balance would be your royalty. You'd save a little on shipping since that would come from the seller's profit.

Choosing a Printer

There are lots of options for printing your book, but if you have a perfect-bound book with a black-and-white interior, POD is going to be your least expensive option.

POD offers access to the book distribution system, which means your book will be available for sale both online and to bookstores at no upfront cost. It erases economy of scale for printing, which means you can order books to sell or give away a few at a time.

There might be a good reason NOT to use POD: you

want a book sized or bound in an unusual way, or you know you can sell large quantities yourself. But for most authors, POD is a dream come true.

At this writing, there are two major POD options. Kindle Direct Publishing (KDP) is Amazon's POD arm, and Ingram Content Group (the country's largest book distributor) offers IngramSpark as a POD vehicle. Both sites have helpful author tools, including royalty calculators, and both offer great advice for book marketing and file prep.

If you expect most of your sales to come online, KDP is probably your best bet. KDP has no file upload fees and offers Amazon distribution. It also has an option for expanded distribution, which makes the book available to other outlets through Ingram. However, KDP's expanded distribution does not offer bookstores a favorable discount rate. IngramSpark charges a fee to set up a title, but for expanded distribution you are allowed to set the discount rate, which means you can offer bookstores the standard discount they expect. IngramSpark also offers Amazon distribution.

Both companies offer color interiors, but IngramSpark is the only option for hardcover books.

Distribution

We discussed metadata and the importance of having your book discovered, but it's also important to have your book in places where it CAN be discovered.

When you upload your files to an online printer, it's important to choose expanded distribution, which will automatically put your book in the distribution system. That means the book will be available on Amazon and other online outlets and to bookstores through Ingram Content Group, which is the largest book distributor in North America. Bookstores can access your book through Ingram, either to stock or for special order.

Ebooks are distributed through KDP, Barnes and Noble Nook publishing, Smashwords, BookBub, and more. Providing the same metadata for your book and ebook will ensure that the book and ebook are linked on online sites.

Ebook Conversion and Sales

Some authors choose just to get an ebook done. That's okay, but it's not much of a shortcut. You still have to put the work into editing and cover design, because that's still how you're going to sell your book.

If you are making a print book, it's relatively easy to make an ebook, too, and it's an important step in the book-making process. Ebooks offer an additional avenue to readers, and allow a great deal of flexibility in terms of pricing and distribution. They are a great and easy tool to use in marketing and can offer opportunities beyond the print book, so don't skip this important step.

Some authors confuse PDFs with ebooks, but though both can be viewed on computer screens, tablets, and mobile devices, they are very different. A PDF is a static document that cannot be changed, and it is not considered a true ebook. A true ebook is a coded file that can be read in multiple formats, offers options such as text size and color, and has reflowable text and a live table of contents.

You can create an ebook from a Word or InDesign file, but it's helpful to understand the basics. Beware of programs that promise to convert with a push of a button. In this case, it's best (and usually relatively inexpensive) to work with someone who understands the HTML coding that will make your ebook look good and work well. Like print books, you want to produce a professional product.

You will need several different types of files. Amazon Kindle uses proprietary software and requires a .mobi file. Most other sites, including Barnes and Noble Nook, use an .epub file.

You can sell your ebook online through many different avenues. KDP and Barnes and Noble Nook Publishing are author-friendly sites. For both, you'll create an account, upload a cover image, fill in the data about your book, and submit your book file.

You can also sell ebooks from your own website or through Smashwords, which is a large distributor of ebooks.

Ebook royalties run between 35 and 65 percent, depending on the price. For Kindle and Nook, pricing your ebook between $2.99 and $9.99 yields the highest royalty. Some sales programs allow you to discount your book or offer it for free during limited periods, and it's worth exploring these marketing options once your book is available.

Finding Your Audience

Book marketing could just as easily have been the first thing we talked about, because if you are self-publishing and hoping for financial return, every step you take along the way should be informed by the need to eventually find an audience to buy your book.

If you've read the previous chapters, you won't be surprised to hear me say that the best marketing tool you can arm yourself with is a good book: a book that is well written and professionally edited with an appropriate and pleasing design. Will a fascinating story and great-looking book guarantee that your book will sell? Unfortunately, it won't. But the inverse is certainly true: if your book is poorly written or edited or looks unprofessional, marketing it will be an uphill battle.

For most writers, marketing is an unappealing and easily ignored part of the process. Writers are generally introverts who prefer to be alone with their thoughts and need plenty of time to capture the perfect turn of phrase on the page. Reaching out to shill a book is the opposite of most writers' dream life.

But book marketing doesn't have to be a scary and onerous prospect—there can be a lot of joy in finding and connecting with an audience, especially one that is thrilled about your work!

There is no perfect or only way to market your book. I'm going to share some conventions to get you started, but you are going to find what works best for you.

First, you must identify your audience. No matter how wonderful your prose, not everyone is a potential reader. You need to think about the person who will be drawn to your book, and think about it very specifically. The more detailed the picture of your typical reader, the better chance that you will be able to find and engage him or her. If you've written a book about women's health, identifying your audience as all women is not going to help you market your book. You need to identify a specific demographic by age, health concerns, maybe marital or parenting status, sexual orientation, and general interest. The better you can figure out the commonalities of your potential readers, the better chance you have of reaching them.

Once you've identified your audience, you can get involved with potential readers by engaging them through social media. You can start building your author platform by positioning yourself as a person with knowledge and interest in a particular subject—the same subjects your potential readers are interested in and which your novel or nonfiction book just happens to be centered around. It's important to note here that your goal is not to join a group and announce immediately that you have written or are writing a book. Most people don't like the hard sale any more than you would. But they do like to converse with interesting, knowledgeable people and will be receptive to your book once you establish yourself as an approachable expert.

You can find like-minded groups by doing some Google searches or searching social media groups that seem to match your topics. Try some different types of social media—Facebook, Twitter, Pinterest, blogs, or Goodreads. Engage in the conversation; find the medium that works for you.

You should also build a local audience. If your book is published or about to be, approach media with suggested stories and things that tie into your book tangentially but are not necessarily book reviews. For instance, a client of mine with a book of her father's WWII letters can position her book beautifully in a story about veterans, particularly near significant anniversaries or national holidays such as Veteran's or Memorial Day.

In addition to press and social media, you should seek out in-person events. Book fairs are great, but it's far more compelling to give a talk about your topic than to read from your book. A great suggestion from one of my authors was to team up with other authors to discuss some aspect of your story or knowledge. Take advantage of your local arts scene and events to offer your services.

As you grow your audience, be sure you have a strategy to build momentum. Collect email wherever you can. Encourage enthusiastic readers to post reviews online. If you speak to a receptive audience, not only should you have a stack of books to sell but you should let them know you are available to speak at other groups, if they know of any, either in person or by Skype. (And always remember to ask the audience for online reviews if they like your work.) Volunteer to speak to book clubs near and far. Follow up on requests and comments both in person and online. One author responded to birthday wishes on social media by saying all she hoped for was a few additional reviews for her book.

Lastly, use the tools that are available: Be sure you are represented everywhere you should be. Make an Amazon author page and keep it up to date. If you have an author website or blog, be sure to post new information on a regular basis. If you're not going to keep a blog current, don't start one. There's nothing worse that being excited about a new author and going to his or her site to find the last post is years old.

At a minimum, you need to have a Facebook page, an email list, and one or two other social media sites. You can set up many of these avenues for free. You should think about where your audience is and how to reach it. You should follow those who are influential or interesting in your genre/field/etc., and comment intelligently and kindly on their posts.

Marketing doesn't have to be the equivalent to standing on a street corner saying *please buy my book*. Think of it more as finding a group of people who are interested in the same things you are.

Here's a way to think about the elements of marketing and how they play into your strategy:

Behind the Scenes:

Book description/back cover text: Be sure this text will draw your reader in. Use keywords in the first paragraph if you can.

Metadata: Populate all the fields you can when you put your book files online: keyword, description, author bio, and BISAC code. Make sure the metadata is consistent across platforms.

Amazon author page: Build one and keep it up to date.

Keywords: Make and keep a list; feel free to use different ones and see what results you get.

Media list/kit: Build a list of media contacts; learn how to write and send a press release; learn how to craft a story pitch

Points of Engagement:

Email list: Collect email whenever you can, and send to your list whenever you have news. Be careful not to overdo it or to have every email be a pitch for a book sale. Offer your fans useful and amusing information to keep them engaged.

Facebook: Build an author or book page, and post regularly. The general rule with social media posts is to keep the heavy sales to about 20 percent of your posts. For the rest, engage your followers, support other authors, and offer useful and amusing information.

Other social media (Twitter, Instagram, etc.): Use any you are comfortable with, and approach them in a way that is similar to newsletters and Facebook.

Blog: If you have something to say, start a blog. If not, forget it. I would suggest a topic tangential to your book as a jumping-off point.

Outreach Strategies:

Blog tour: You can set up a virtual tour for your book by contacting other bloggers and offering to host or write as a guest blogger.

Book clubs: Offer to visit clubs in person or by Skype to engage new readers.

Speaking engagements: Look for opportunities to speak in front of civic groups, at book fairs, or other places about your book or topics related to it.

Articles: Seek print publications or online sites that accept writing on topics related to your book. Your author bio should mention the title of your book, giving you a chance to reach new readers.

Glossary

Below is a list of terms you will become familiar with as you embark on your publishing venture. This is by no means comprehensive but is included as a quick reference for newly independent authors.

Self-publishing: When an author assumes the role of publisher for his or her own work, assuming the financial risk and taking on the duties of publisher. Also referred to as indie publishing.

Print-on-demand (POD): A book printing system that uses high-quality PDF files to print and bind books only as they are ordered. Most self-publishing authors use POD to publish and distribute their books.

Metadata: Information about a particular book that allows the book to be identified correctly. Metadata often includes but is not limited to: the book title, subtitle, author, ISBN, Library of Congress number, book dimensions, and book description.

Distribution: A system for getting books from printer to reader, usually through a third-party sales outlet such as a bookstore or online site like Amazon.

Royalty payments: The portion of a book sale that an author receives. For POD books, the royalty is what remains after the cost of printing and the retail discount given to a third-party seller are subtracted from the retail price.

Third-party sellers: Retail outlets, both online and brick and mortar, who sell your book to readers through their sales channels. Third-party sellers will take a cut of the retail price of each book.

Ebook: A book that is delivered in electronic format to a device. Some ebook formats are suitable only for a particular device; many cross platforms and are available on a wide range of devices.

Genre: The specific category that defines a book. Genres include romance, horror, memoir, science fiction, and much more.

Manuscript: The body of writing that will become a book.

POD book: A bound book whose interior pages and cover are printed from high-quality PDFs.

Font: A set of text characters in a specific style and size.

Keywords: Words that are often embedded in online sites and are used by search engines to find related material.

Front and back matter: Book text other than the main body of the text. This can include such things as copyright page, dedication, title page, table of contents, index, acknowledgments, author biography, bibliography, and author note.

Book block: The interior pages of a book with all text intended to be printed for the book.

Sales discount: The percentage the retail price is discounted for third-party sellers.

Blurb: A quote (often of praise) used on the cover or inside of the book. Blurbs generally come from other authors or experts in the field.

Formatting: The process of arranging text to create a book page, applying special effects or styles such as bold or italic to text.

Portable document format (PDF): PDFs are the output for many design programs.

Proof: A printed version of a book, often reviewed by the author as a last step before publishing.

Resources

Editing

Editorial Freelancers Association - www.the-efa.org/
American Copy Editors Society - www.copydesk.org/
Northwest Independent Editors Guild - edsguild.org/

Ebook Publishing

Kindle Direct Publishing - kdp.amazon.com/en_US/
Nook Press - www.nookpress.com/
BookBub - www.bookbub.com/home/
Smashwords - www.smashwords.com/

Print-on-Demand Publishing

Kindle Direct Publishing - kdp.amazon.com/en_US/
IngramSpark - www.ingramspark.com

MetaData

Bowker Books in Print - www.myidentifiers.com/
Library of Congress -
    ecips.loc.gov/pls/ecip/pubs_signon?system=pcn/

Photo Sites

123rf - www.123rf.com/
Shutterstock - www.shutterstock.com/home/
Wikimedia Commons -
    commons.wikimedia.org/wiki/Main_Page/
iStockPhotos - www.istockphoto.com/
Adobe Stock - stock.adobe.com/

About the Author

 **PATRICIA MARSHALL** is the owner of Luminare Press. She has helped hundreds of authors navigate the self-publishing process and enjoys sharing her knowledge, enthusiasm, and love of publishing with authors across the country.

Patricia is the former editor of *Forest Magazine*, a conservation magazine published by a national environmental group located in Eugene. She has a degree in journalism from the University of Oregon, an MFA in creative nonfiction from Goucher College in Baltimore, and a certificate in digital journalism from Media Bistro in New York. She is a member of the Northwest Editors Guild and the Eugene Chamber of Commerce and is active in civic events.

Patricia also serves as the board chair of Wordcrafters in Eugene, a literary nonprofit. Wordcrafters hosts an annual writing conference, has a Writers in the Schools program, and offers year-round literary events and classes to writers of all ages in the Eugene/Springfield area.

For more information about publishing, or to
schedule a free consultation, contact
www.luminarepress.com
541-636-3102
info@luminarepress.com

Made in the
USA
Lexington, KY